Acknowledgments
The editor and publishers would like to thank Mary Haselden for her help in selecting rhymes for this book and Sue Raffe, who wrote *I climbed to the top of the slide in the park; High, low, high; Under my umbrella; There are some times when I'm so sad; There was a bad fairy; Mummy closed the curtains; Up and up the hill we climb* and *When my tummy rumbles.*

British Library Cataloguing in Publication Data

Opposites.
    1. English language. Antonyms – For children
    I. Chamberlain, Margaret   428.1
    ISBN 0-7214-1178-9

First edition

Published by Ladybird Books Ltd Loughborough Leicestershire UK
Ladybird Books Inc Auburn Maine 04210 USA

Printed in England

opposites

illustrated by MARGARET CHAMBERLAIN

Ladybird Books

little

A little mouse lived in a hole
Down by the kitchen door.
The mouse came out to
              look for crumbs
All on the kitchen floor.

As he was busy nibbling crumbs
Out jumped a big fat cat.
So off ran mousie
              back to his hole
And that was the end of that.

small

Small and round,
Small and round,
The bulb is deep
Inside the ground.

Stretch and grow,
Stretch and grow,
Up the stalk comes,
Slow, slow, slow.

The buds unfurl,
The buds unfurl,
See the petals
Outward curl.

tall

Straight and tall,
Straight and tall,
The flowers grow
Against the garden wall.

on

Polly put the kettle on,
Polly put the kettle on,
Polly put the kettle on,
We'll all have tea.

off

Sukey take it off again,
Sukey take it off again,
Sukey take it off again,
They've all gone away.

top

I climbed to the top of the slide
in the park,
Up high, I felt ever so small.
Right at the top, my knees
started to knock,
And I thought I was going to fall.

bottom

So Mummy climbed to me;
　　　　I sat on her lap
And down to the bottom we came.
Then back to the top of the slide
　　　　we both climbed
And slid down together again.

Tall shop in the town,
Lifts moving up and down;
Doors swinging round about,
People walking in and out.

Little Jack Horner
Sat in the corner,
Eating a Christmas pie;
He put in his thumb,
And pulled out a plum,
And said, ''What a good boy am I!''

high

High, low, high,
My friend and I
Swing low near
the ground
And high to the sky.

A tiny, tiny worm
Wriggled along the ground;
It wriggled along like so
Ever so, ever so low.
It came to a tiny hole,
A tiny hole in the ground;
It wriggled right inside
Without a sound.

Under my umbrella,
I shelter from the rain;
It splashes all around my feet
And trickles down the drain.

Under my umbrella,
My head and arms stay dry;
Sometimes my legs get very wet
When cars go splashing by.

Hey diddle, diddle,
The cat and the fiddle,
The cow jumped over the moon;
The little dog laughed
To see such fun,
And the dish ran away
With the spoon.

straight

I'm a soldier
straight and strong,
See the way
I march along.

I'm an old man
rather bent,
Can you see
the way I went?

But together
we can go
Much more easily,
fast or slow.

crooked

There was a crooked man,
And he walked a crooked mile;
He found a crooked sixpence
Against a crooked stile;
He bought a crooked cat,
Which caught a crooked mouse,
And they all lived together
In a little crooked house.

sad

There are some times
      when I'm so sad,
It makes me want to cry;
Like when I'm very tired or ill,
Or clouds appear above the hill
And rain pours from the sky.

happy

But most times I am happy,
And I laugh and shout with glee;
Like when my granny
                    comes to stay,
Or when I have my friends to play
And favourite food for tea.

lost

Lucy Locket lost her pocket,
Kitty Fisher found it;
Not a penny was there in it,
Only ribbon round it.

Jennie Muddlecombe has lost
                    her hat.
She can't find it anywhere,
                    well fancy that!
She walked down the high street
                    and everyone said,
"Funny Jennie Muddlecombe,
                    her hat is on her head!"

bad

There was a bad fairy
Who cast wicked spells,
She sprayed people's flowers
With horrible smells.

She made little girls trip
And fall on their knees;
She had little boys stung
By big buzzing bees.

She tried out a new spell
To make people sick,
But she made a mistake
With this nasty trick.

good

She turned very spotty
And itchy and red;
She felt very ill
And she went home to bed.

A good fairy made sure
That she became well,
By using a very strong,
VERY GOOD spell.

And then the bad fairy
Became very good,
And cast helpful, good spells
Whenever she could.

Puffer train, puffer train,
Noisy little puffer train.
If you're going to the sea,
Puffer train, oh please take me!
Ff-Ff-Ff, Sh-Sh-Sh,
Ch-Ch-Ch-Ch-Ch, Ch-Ch-Ch,
Noisy little puffer train.

A mouse lived in a little hole,
Lived softly in a little hole;
When all was quiet as quiet can be
    (Sh! Sh!),
When all was quiet as quiet can be
    (Sh! Sh!),
Out popped HE!

rainy

I hear thunder,
I hear thunder;
Hark don't you?
Hark don't you?
Pitter-patter raindrops,
Pitter-patter raindrops,
I'm wet through,
SO ARE YOU!

I see blue skies,
I see blue skies,
Way up high,
Way up high,
Hurry up the sunshine,
Hurry up the sunshine,
I'll soon dry,
I'll soon dry.

closed

Mummy closed the curtains,
Mummy closed the door;
Little children closed their eyes
And slept without a snore.

Some had dreams of toy shops,
Some dreamed they could fly;
Some had dreams of nasty things
That made them want to cry.

open

Morning came and opened eyes
For another day.
Doors and curtains opened too,
For it was time to play.

up

Up and up the hill we climb,
Sometimes we have to stop.
Then, puffing, up we climb again
Until we reach the top.

down

Down the hill we slip and slide,
By sitting on a tray.
Down at the bottom
          we fall in the snow,
It's soft and deep today.

slowly

Slowly, slowly, very slowly
Creeps the garden snail;
Slowly, slowly, very slowly
Up the wooden rail.

quickly

Quickly, quickly, very quickly
Runs the little mouse;
Quickly, quickly, very quickly
Round about the house.

empty

When my tummy rumbles,
I know it's time for tea;
It's saying, "Come on, fill me up,
I'm empty as can be."

full

So then I fill my tummy,
But if I eat a lot,
It blows up like a big balloon
And nearly goes off POP!

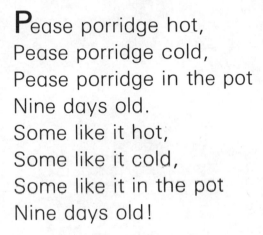

Pease porridge hot,
Pease porridge cold,
Pease porridge in the pot
Nine days old.
Some like it hot,
Some like it cold,
Some like it in the pot
Nine days old!

asleep

This little girl is ready for bed,
On her pillow she lays her head,
Wraps herself in her blanket tight,
Closes her eyes and says,

"Goodnight."

awake

Morning comes, she opens her eyes,
Back with a toss the blanket flies.
Up she gets, dresses and away,
Down to the nursery school to play.

Mrs Pin is very thin,
Mr Pratt is very fat,
Mrs Court is very short,
Mrs Hall is very tall,

Mr Dent is very bent,
Mr Wait is very straight,
Mrs Mould is very old,
Mrs Bung is very young.